Get Art Smart

What Is Space?

by Susan Markowitz Meredith

Crabtree Publishing Company
www.crabtreebooks.com

Crabtree Publishing Company

Author: Susan Meredith
Publishing plan research and development: Sean Charlebois, Reagan Miller Crabtree Publishing Company
Editors: Reagan Miller
Proofreader: Kathy Middleton, Molly Aloian
Editorial director: Kathy Middleton
Photo research: Edward A. Thomas
Designer: Tammy West, Westgraphix LLC
Production coordinator: Margaret Amy Salter
Prepress technician: Margaret Amy Salter
Consultant: Julie Collins-Dutkiewicz, B.A., specialist in early childhood education, Sandy Waite, M.Ed., U.S. National Board Certified Teacher, author, and literacy consultant
Reading Consultant: Susan Nations, M.Ed., Author/Literacy Coach/Consultant in Literacy Development

Photographs and reproductions
Cover: Shutterstock; 1: Shuttersotock; 5: iStockphoto; 7, 9: Image Club Graphics: Circa Art; 11: Museo Marciano, Basilica di San Marco, Venice, Italy/Cameraphoto Arte Venezia/ The Bridgeman Art Library; 13: Private Collection/Peter Willi/The Bridgeman Art Library; 15: The Iveagh Bequest, Kenwood House, London/The Bridgeman Art Library; 17: Art Institute of Chicago/The Bridgeman Art Library; 19: Private Collection/The Bridgeman Art Library; 21: National Gallery of Art, Washington, D.C./The Bridgeman Art Library; 23: illustration by Tammy West.

Front cover (main image): A girl playing hopscotch in a drawn landscape.
Title page: A young girl creating a pillar of building blocks.

Written, developed, and produced by RJF Publishing LLC

Library and Archives Canada Cataloguing in Publication

Meredith, Susan, 1951-
What is space? / Susan Markowitz Meredith.

(Get art smart)
Includes index.
ISBN 978-0-7787-5126-7 (bound).--ISBN 978-0-7787-5140-3 (pbk.)

1. Space (Art)--Juvenile literature. I. Title. II. Series: Get art smart

N7430.7.M47 2009 j701'.8 C2009-903590-1

Library of Congress Cataloging-in-Publication Data

Meredith, Susan, 1951-

What is space? / Susan Markowitz Meredith.
p. cm. -- (Get art smart)
Includes index.
ISBN 978-0-7787-5140-3 (pbk. : alk. paper) -- ISBN 978-0-7787-5126-7 (reinforced library binding : alk. paper)
1. Space (Art)--Juvenile literature. I. Title.

N7430.7.M47 2009
701'.8--dc22

2009023307

Crabtree Publishing Company
www.crabtreebooks.com 1-800-387-7650

In Canada: We acknowledge the financial support of the Government of Canada through the Book Publishing Industry Development Program (BPIDP) for our publishing activities.

Published in Canada
Crabtree Publishing
616 Welland Ave.
St. Catharines, Ontario
L2M 5V6

Published in the United States
Crabtree Publishing
PMB16A
350 Fifth Ave., Suite 3308
New York, NY 10118

Published in the United Kingdom
Crabtree Publishing
Maritime House
Basin Road North, Hove
BN41 1WR

Published in Australia
Crabtree Publishing
386 Mt. Alexander Rd.
Ascot Vale (Melbourne)
VIC 3032

Contents

What Is Space?

Classrooms are filled with things. There are desks and chairs. There are bookcases full of books, too. But something else is between the objects. It is an empty area we call **space**. Every room has space inside it. Even outside, there is space around objects.

Space is around the people and things in this classroom.

Space in Art

There is space in every work of art. We just have to look for it. In a picture, space is around the lines and shapes. Sometimes space seems to be behind the shapes. Sometimes it is in front.

On the Beach at Boulogne, by Edouard Manet (1868)

Space is in front of the people in this picture. Space is also behind them.

Taking Up Space

Shapes that look thick take up their own space in a picture. Each of these shapes is called a **form**. Forms can be people, animals, plants, and buildings. They may also be everyday objects like plates and food.

Still Life with Decanter and Lemons on a Plate, by Vincent van Gogh (1887)

Look at the fruit, the plate, and the bottle of water. They take up their own space in this picture.

Clay, Stone, and More

Works of art made of clay, stone, metal, or wood also take up space. Forms like these are called **sculptures**. Big sculptures take up a lot of space. Small sculptures take up just a little. There is space around every sculpture, too.

The Four Horses of San Marco, probably made in the second or third century A.D.

These sculptures are made of metal.

Space in a Picture

We can create space in different ways when we make art. Sometimes shapes stand out in a picture. They look closer to us. Our eyes want to look at them first.

Madame Monet on a Garden Bench, by Claude Monet (1873)

Notice the woman on the bench and the man next to her. They stand out in this picture.

Behind and In Front

Sometimes the space in a picture looks like it goes far back. How can we make space go far back when we create art? Some artists put shapes partly on top of each other. The shapes in front **overlap** the ones behind them. The shapes that are partly covered up look far away.

The Guitar Player, by Jan Vermeer (1672)

In this picture, the woman's head partly covers up the painting on the wall. The painting looks like it is far back.

Size and Space

We can also make space look like it goes far back by creating shapes of different **sizes**. We can paint some people larger and other people smaller. The larger people look closer to us than the smaller ones. In real life, faraway objects also look smaller.

Sunday Afternoon on the Island of La Grande Jatte, by Georges Seurat (1884)

The larger people in this picture look closer to us.

Higher and Lower

We can place objects high or low in a picture to make them look far away or close. We place objects that we want to look close lower down in the picture. Mountains are high up in many pictures because the artist wants them to look far away. They are in the **distance**.

A Seascape, by Ando Hiroshige (1853)

The mountain is high up in this picture. It looks far away.

Making Space Flat

Some artists do not make the space in their pictures look like it goes far back. They make the space look flat. All the lines and shapes seem to be next to each other. None of them stands out or seems to be far back.

Little Girl in Lavender, by John Bradley (1840)

The space in this picture looks flat.

A Different Space

Sometimes we can use black and white to make the space in pictures look different. Look at the pictures on the next page. First, look at the white spaces. Next, look at the black spaces. Do you see faces? Do you see a vase?

First, look at the white spaces. Then, look at the black spaces. Do you see different things?

Words to Know

distance

form

overlap

sculpture

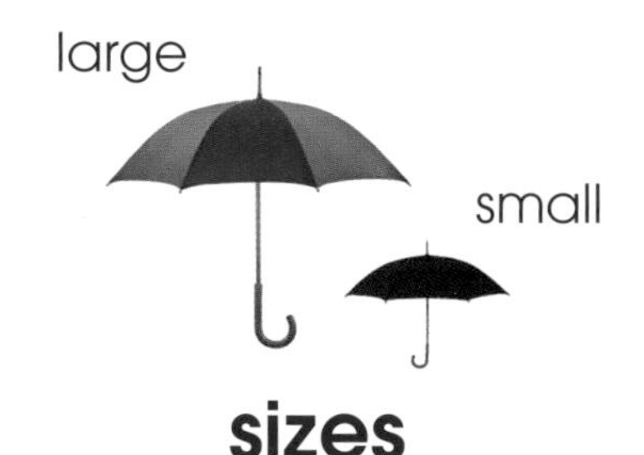

sizes

space

Find Out More

Books

Cressy, Judith. *Can You Find It?* New York: Harry N. Abrams, 2002.

Raczka, Bob. *Art Is…* Brookfield, CT: Millbrook Press, 2003.

Web sites

Art Games
www.albrightknox.org/artgames/html/Gris/index.html

Getty Games
www.getty.edu/gettygames/jigsaw

Printed in the USA—CG